WILLIAM & KATE

TO COMMEMORATE THE ENGAGEMENT OF PRINCE WILLIAM OF WALES
AND MISS CATHERINE MIDDLETON, 16 NOVEMBER 2010

WILLIAM & KATE

ANNIE BULLEN

Frontispiece: Arm in arm the engaged couple pose for photographers in the Entrée Room of St James's Palace.

Title page: Prince William and Kate Middleton smile happily as they announce their engagement at St James's Palace.

The moral right of the author has been asserted.
Written by Annie Bullen.

The author wishes to thank Brian Hoey for information used from his book *Prince William*.

Editorial consultant Brian Hoey. The publisher would like to thank Brian Hoey for writing the Foreword and for his editorial guidance.

Edited by Shelley Grimwood.
Picture research by Jan Kean.
Cover designed by Katie Beard.
Designed by Glad Stockdale.
Production by Karen Kinnear.

A CIP catalogue for this book is available from the British Library.
Published by Pitkin Publishing, Healey House, Dene Road, Andover, Hampshire, SP10 2AA
www.pitkin-guides.com

Printed in Great Britain.
ISBN 978-1-84165-353-2   1/11

CONTENTS

FOREWORD

Prince William and Catherine Middleton, known to the world as Kate, are perfect examples of a young generation that proves one's origins do not matter when love is involved.

The Middletons could be described as the face of modern Britain, hard-working, self-made and entrepreneurial: a middle-class family who have successfully bridged the gap between their modest origins and royalty.

William and Catherine are the products of prestigious public schools – Eton and Marlborough – and an equally exclusive university, St Andrews, where each gained an impressive upper second-class degree.

They have not rushed into marriage, having built their relationship over several years, and so their love has blossomed out of a feeling of true companionship, which in turn points to a long-lasting and loving commitment.

They share many interests and enjoy a mutual understanding that is the basis for every successful marriage. In other words, they are not just in love, they are also the best of friends.

The couple have captured the public's attention in a way not seen since William's mother, the late Diana, Princess of Wales, arrived on the royal scene in 1981. The manner in which they have accomplished this is in complete contrast to the former reverential image of royalty when the mere mention of their names was spoken in hushed tones.

Today, William, with his boyish good looks, undoubted charm and self-deprecating sense of humour, and Catherine, whose natural beauty and outgoing personality make her a photographer's dream, generate an impression of royalty that is a formidable combination of star quality and an approachable common touch.

William's life has been mapped out from the moment he was born. He is a king-in-waiting, and his education and subsequent career to date have been part of his ongoing training as a future monarch. He accepts this as an inevitable part of his destiny. It is the job for which he will be best qualified –

and for which he is the only applicant. As The Queen's grandson, he displays that Windsor streak of strong self-discipline when it is needed. He may be considered to be one of the most informal royals of recent years; however if and when the occasion demands it, he can be as traditional and conventional as every other member of the most famous family in the world. Nobody forgets for a moment who he is and what his role is. Nevertheless, William has been more fortunate than previous princes in his position in that he has enjoyed much more freedom – to choose his own friends, visit theatres and restaurants and meet people from all walks of life. And because of this, he has been able to develop an independence formerly unknown amongst royalty.

Catherine's different background is seen as a definite advantage. She comes from a stable family who have welcomed Prince William to their home and, he says, given him a glimpse of the kind of happiness he hopes to share in the years to come. Catherine is one of the most natural women one could possibly know: outgoing, gregarious and with a friendly laugh that disarms everyone who meets her for the first time. She brings into the Royal Family grace and dignity along with her undoubted beauty and intelligence. William recognized these qualities the first time they met and he says that one of the things he finds so appealing and attractive in his fiancée is their shared sense of humour – something they may come to rely on in the years to come.

William and Catherine are the new, modern face of royalty. Together they will ensure the continued stability of the monarchy when the time comes for Prince William to ascend the throne. In the interim they hope to be able to enjoy many years of married life as a comparatively normal couple, albeit surrounded by police protection at all times.

Nobody influenced William in his choice of bride. There is no political or monarchical expediency required these days when a royal spouse is selected.

This was entirely the young couple's own decision. They decided if and when they were to be married, without interference from anyone.

Catherine's introduction to life as a member of the Royal Family will be carried out with the utmost care and consideration, so that she may move seamlessly into the role she will play within 'The Firm' – the name King George VI bestowed on the immediate Royal Family over 60 years ago.

As a princess, Catherine will be required to undertake public duties as a matter of course, but her prime responsibility in the early years will be as wife to a serving officer in the Royal Air Force.

Those who witnessed the television interview the couple gave on 16 November 2010, the day their engagement was announced will have noticed how protective William is towards Catherine and, in the months to come, his advice and guidance will be invaluable in helping her prepare for life under the continuous scrutiny of the media and the public.

As an intelligent and articulate young woman who knows her own mind, Catherine will surely already have some idea of the part she would like to play in their future. She has an unshakeable belief in the monarchy and, realistically, she and William understand that she will become a role model for young women throughout the world. Catherine has already shown that she possesses the strength of character she will need in the days and years to come.

Catherine's personal style is already being copied by many young women of her generation. Whether she likes it or not, she will become a fashion icon, with everything she wears subjected to microscopic examination and criticism. She looks charming and has a quite natural grace, an enviable figure and as recent pictures have shown, the camera loves her. So she starts out with a huge advantage.

There is a groundswell of public goodwill towards William and Catherine that should continue to encourage them as they prepare for their life together.

Once they realize and accept that public interest in the Royal Family is inexhaustible and the curiosity is well-intentioned, they will reach an understanding of why we are so obsessed with their everyday lives.

The royal wedding on 29 April 2011 will be a cause for celebration for the entire nation and the wider world, and the couple have expressed their hopes that everyone will join them in their celebrations.

Prince William and Catherine are the stars of the future, the jewels in the royal crown, on whose shoulders rest the hopes for the British monarchy. Together they are a priceless asset for the Royal Family and the country.

We wish them every happiness.

Brian Hoey

DATES & EVENTS

1982 Kate Middleton and Prince William were born; Miss Middleton at the Royal Berkshire Hospital, Reading, Berkshire on 9 January, the Prince on 21 June at the private Lindo Wing of St Mary's Hospital, Paddington, London.

1985 William's first day at school; the decision to send him to a nursery school broke with royal tradition.

1991 The young Prince William undertakes an early public engagement when he accompanies his parents, Prince Charles and Princess Diana, on a visit to Llandaff Cathedral to celebrate St David's Day.

1995 Prince William, as 'William Wales', goes to Eton College, in Berkshire. Kate Middleton is a pupil at Marlborough College in Wiltshire.

2000–01 Both William and Kate opt for 'gap years' before university. Although they did not meet, Kate worked at a project in Chile in 2001 where Prince William had been a month earlier.

2001 William and Kate meet at St Andrews University, where they are both studying Art History; they have rooms close to each other in St Salvator's Hall.

2002 In March, William buys a £200 ticket to a charity fashion show and is impressed by Kate's appearance on the catwalk.

2002 In September, they move into a student flat in Hope Street, St Andrews, with two other friends.

2003 In May, newspapers publish photographs of William and Kate deep in conversation at a rugby match.

2003 Kate is a guest at William's 21st birthday party at Windsor Castle; in September, they move into a cottage, for their third year at university.

2004 The couple are pictured together on the ski slopes at Klosters, Switzerland.

2005 In June, Kate joins William for the wedding of his friend Hugh van Cutsem; the couple graduate from St Andrews.

2005   The couple fly to Kenya for a holiday at the Lewa Downs game reserve.

2006   Prince William is photographed for the first time kissing Kate, during another skiing holiday at Klosters in January.

2006   In January, Prince William starts his army training at Sandhurst.

2006   In May, Kate is invited to the wedding of Laura Parker Bowles, the Prince's step sister.

2006   In November, Kate begins work as an accessories buyer for fashion chain Jigsaw.

2006   In December, Kate is invited to Sandhurst to watch William graduate as an army officer.

2007   Prince William starts army training in Dorset. In March, William and Kate are photographed together watching the Cheltenham Gold Cup.

2007   In April, it is confirmed that William and Kate have split up; by June there are rumours that they are back together again.

2007   In October, they are photographed out on the town together and Kate is invited to Balmoral for the weekend.

2008   In April, Kate is at the Prince's side as he graduates from the RAF at Cranwell.

2008   In June, for the first time Kate appears at a formal royal public occasion when she attends the Order of the Garter Service at Windsor Castle to watch William's investiture.

2008   William and Kate enjoy a holiday at Birkhall, the Prince of Wales's private hunting lodge on the Balmoral estate.

2009   In May, the couple are photographed together at a polo match.

2010   William and Kate take a New Year break at Birkhall.

2010   In January, Kate watches as William graduates from an advanced helicopter flying course, receiving his wings from his father, the Prince of Wales.

2010   In March, the couple join Kate's parents on holiday in Courchevel, France.

2010   On 16 November a brief statement is released from Clarence House announcing William and Kate's engagement.

A ROYAL
Engagement

The announcement, from Clarence House, just after 11 o'clock on Tuesday 16 November 2010, was matter-of-fact, but its joyful impact was felt by a nation hungry for a genuine love story. And there could be no doubt in any mind that this was the real thing.

Kate Middleton took Prince William's arm as they walked into the red and gold grandeur of the Entrée Room at St James's Palace to face the world's media. Love shone through every gesture, each exchanged glance and every movement towards each other as the young couple, standing closely together under royal portraits, told of their happiness and their plans for the future.

Prince William and his wife-to-be had known each other since 2001 and had spent years preparing for this occasion. But the news, when it came, was still a happy surprise and a moment of both public hope and private joy.

The Prince and Kate Middleton, both smiling with happiness, gave the impression of a couple completely at ease together, not frightened to touch or hold hands or gently tease each other in public.

'The Prince of Wales is delighted to announce the engagement of Prince William to Miss Catherine Middleton. Prince William and Miss Middleton became engaged in October during a private holiday in Kenya. Prince William has informed The Queen and other close members of his family. Prince William has also sought the permission of Miss Middleton's father. Following the marriage, the couple will live in North Wales, where Prince William will continue to serve with the Royal Air Force.'

Left: Kate's deep-sapphire blue dress was a perfect match for her engagement ring.

Above: A loving look passes between the happy couple as they tell
the world of their plans to marry.

Prominent on Kate's perfectly manicured left hand was the glorious sapphire and diamond ring that Prince William's mother, the late Princess Diana, had worn when her engagement to the Prince of Wales was announced almost 30 years ago.

And Kate, facing her first formal public appearance with her royal fiancé, emerged with credit from this daunting debut. Unlike Diana, who came from an aristocratic family, this newest recruit to the Royal Family is a middle-class woman. But she coped confidently with the media attention on the first day of the rest of her life.

She admitted that the prospect of joining the Royal Family was a daunting one.

'Hopefully I'll take it in my stride,' she said, turning towards the Prince. 'And William's a great teacher, so hopefully he'll be able to help me along the way.'

'He's treated me very well, as the loving boyfriend he is. Over the years William has looked after me. He is very supportive of me through the good times and also through the bad times.'

Prince William had no doubts about their compatibility: 'We both have a fun time together, both have a very good sense of humour, we're down to earth, we take the mickey out of each other a lot, and she's got plenty of habits that make me laugh that I tease her about.'

Left: Smiling for the cameras. The engagement was announced amid the grandeur of St James's Palace.

He is heir presumptive, second in line to the throne, our future King, brought up with every privilege that accrues to royalty.

She comes from a wealthy middle-class family, no different from many others whose children are privately educated and brought up in comfortable homes, rather than from the elite aristocracy from whose circles William might have been expected to choose a bride.

His family background is understandably more formal, bound by duty, tradition and royal protocol. He lost his beloved mother in a tragic accident when he was just 15.

Her family is close-knit, her parents Carole and Michael giving Kate and her siblings, Pippa and James, a happy and comfortable childhood in the Home Counties.

Both Prince William and Kate have had time over their long friendship and romance to get to know their prospective in-laws – a relationship more daunting for the bride-to-be than the Prince. But although Kate admits that she was nervous about meeting Prince Charles, William's father, her fears were unfounded. She says that he was 'very, very welcoming, very friendly' and the meeting could not have gone more easily. Meeting William's grandmother, Her Majesty Queen Elizabeth II, must have been an equally daunting prospect, but the introduction happened at the wedding of Peter Phillips, son of Princess Anne, the Princess Royal, in 2008 and she was also, says Kate, 'very friendly'.

The Queen expressed delight at the news of her grandson's engagement in an official statement and privately admitted her joy at the 'brilliant' news, which had 'taken them a very long time'. Prince Charles, too, said he was thrilled and, in a characteristic display of dry humour, added: 'they've been practising long enough.' William's step mother, the Duchess of Cornwall, was just as forthright when she heard the news. Clearly delighted, she told reporters: 'I'm just so happy and so are they. It's wicked!'

William, too, has said that he has grown very fond of Kate's family. 'Kate's got a very, very close family. I get on really well with them and I'm very lucky that they've been so supportive. Mike and Carole have been really loving and caring, and really fun and have been really welcoming towards me, so I've felt really a part of the family.'

And Kate's parents have clearly taken their future son-in-law to their hearts, describing him as 'wonderful'. 'Catherine and Prince William have been going out together for quite a number of years, which is great for us because we have got to know William very well. We all think he is wonderful and we are extremely fond of him,' said Kate's father Michael from his home at Bucklebury, near Newbury in Berkshire, as news of the engagement was released.

Above: Michael and Carole Middleton, Kate's parents, smile with delight as the news of their daughter's engagement is announced.

Above: Queen Elizabeth and Prince Philip, William's grandparents, pictured here in New York in 2010, said they were delighted with news of the engagement.

When William and Kate shared their happy news with a delighted world, her arm tucked through his as she leaned towards him, no one who saw them could have failed to notice the beautiful sapphire, surrounded by 14 brilliant-cut diamonds, set in a white-gold band on the third finger of her left hand.

Kate's oval engagement ring, now one of the most famous gems in the world, is of huge sentimental value to Prince William and of more-than-usual emotional significance to the happy couple. It was the ring given to the Prince's mother, then Lady Diana Spencer, by Prince Charles when he proposed 29 years ago.

William, who inherited the ring from his mother's estate after her death in 1997, showed that it was priceless to him by choosing to present it to his fiancée as she accepted his proposal of marriage.

'It's very special to me,' William told the world as cameras homed in on the sparkling ring, which fitted Kate perfectly without alteration. 'Kate is very special to me now as well, and it is only right that the two are put together. It was my way of making sure that my mother didn't miss out on today, and the excitement and the fact that we're going to spend the rest of our lives together.'

The Prince also revealed that he had proposed to Kate while they were on holiday in Kenya and that he had carried the ring with him, safely tucked into a pocket in his rucksack, never daring to let it out of his sight. 'I literally would not let it go,' he said. 'Everywhere I went I was keeping hold of it because I knew if it disappeared I would be in a lot of trouble.'

Above: Princess Elizabeth and Prince Philip announced their engagement in 1947.

Left: Kate's engagement ring holds special memories: it was given to William's mother, Princess Diana on her engagement to Prince Charles.

Left: Kate's engagement ring is a beautiful sapphire, surrounded by 14 brilliant-cut diamonds, set in a white-gold band.

Below: Kate, smiling happily, is composed as she faces the world's press.

Kate's engagement ring was considered unconventional when Lady Diana Spencer chose it from a tray of gems sent for her selection on the occasion of her engagement to Prince Charles. Diamonds are traditionally the centrepiece of an engagement ring. Princess Diana's ring cost £28,000 and, although it was not made specifically for her, it was unusual and beautiful. She is said to have chosen it because she loved sapphires, which at one time were thought to exude heavenly rays.

Inevitably the sight of the ring raised questions about Kate's attitude towards the extraordinary legacy of the late Princess of Wales. Did she find it intimidating and was there pressure to step into her shoes? Kate admitted that she would have loved to have met William's mother: 'She was obviously an inspirational woman to look up to on this day,' she said.

William, protective towards Kate, was quick to insist that there would be no pressure for his future wife to take over Diana's role: 'You know it's about carving your own future. No one is trying to fill my mother's shoes.'

'What she did is fantastic. It's about making your own future and your own destiny and Kate will do a very good job of that,' he said.

When Prince William and Kate Middleton flew out to Kenya in October 2010 she had no idea that this was anything more than a three-week holiday to see spectacular wildlife and enjoy some time together in the seclusion of the African bush.

Africa occupies a special place in the heart of the Prince, who found solace in its wild spaces after the death of his mother Princess Diana in 1997, when his father took him and his brother Harry to Kenya to recuperate. Some years later, during his gap year, William visited Kenya again to enjoy a happy eight months working in the north of the country.

But the October visit was different. Tucked away in his rucksack was the symbol of his love, his late mother's sapphire and diamond ring, which he planned to put on Kate's finger if she agreed to become his wife.

They spent some time with friends, in tents in the bush – home to lions, elephants and rhino – before moving to a luxury hill-top home on a 55,000-acre (22,000-hectare) nature reserve with wide-ranging views across the African savannah. Their days were filled with driving out to see the animals roaming the plains, while they enjoyed the company of friends in the evenings. They visited a luxury tented camp where they watched giraffe, wild dogs, elephant and buffalo come to a nearby waterhole to drink. And still Kate had no idea of William's ulterior motive for this special holiday.

But, just before the end of the visit, William borrowed a tough vehicle and drove to the beautiful shores of the Rutundu Lake, high on the slopes of Mount Kenya, where the couple stayed in a romantic wooden lodge with a wide veranda overlooking the beautiful scenery which has been likened to that of Scotland, with its views to snow-topped peaks and heather-covered hills.

It was here that the Prince asked Kate to be his wife. And it was here that she accepted his proposal and the pledge of his affection, the sapphire ring that had once belonged to his mother.

Neither William nor Kate would reveal any details of the proposal, refusing to say if William had gone down on one knee when he put the question. Kate would only say: 'It was very romantic and it was very personal. There's a true romantic in there.'

Mount Kenya was the dramatic backdrop to another important moment in the history of the Royal Family. The Queen was staying at the Treetops Lodge in Aberdare's National Park in February 1952, when the sad news of the death of her father King George VI came through. It was here that she learnt that she had succeeded to the throne as Queen Elizabeth II.

Prince William makes his own decisions and it is a measure of his strength of character that he kept his engagement secret for almost four weeks, only telling his grandmother The Queen and his father Prince Charles the day before the happy news was released to the world.

William revealed that he did actually ask Kate's father Michael Middleton for his daughter's hand in marriage – but he waited until Kate had accepted his proposal.

'I was torn between asking Kate's father first and then the realization that he might actually say "no" dawned. So I thought, "If I ask Kate first, he can't really say no". So I did it that way.'

Right: The couple stand happily side by side for press photographs at St James's Palace.

A ROYAL *Wedding*

Although Kate Middleton and Prince William have insisted they want to be in control on their big day, they won't have to worry about the thousand and one details with which most brides and bridegrooms have to cope. The royal pair will hand the bulk of the planning over to the Palace's team of wedding organizers who are certain to put on a fabulous event and be meticulous over every detail of a splendid occasion.

Heads of state, royalty, politicians, celebrities and members of Britain's oldest families will be on the guest list alongside more 'ordinary' people. William and Kate have asked aides to include those who have made a contribution to life in Britain, perhaps through the charities that the Royal Family supports.

The Household of Prince William and Prince Harry at Clarence House, where the Princes' private secretary, Jamie Lowther-Pinkerton – a former SAS officer – runs their private office, will head the wedding arrangements with plenty of support from the Lord Chamberlain's Office and the Prince of Wales's Household.

Friday 29 April 2011 is the day that one-sixth of all people on earth are expected to tune in for the wedding of Britain's future King and Queen. A public holiday has been announced and it is likely that whole neighbourhoods will celebrate with street parties, concerts and impromptu get-togethers.

The wedding will be planned with the knowledge that we live in times of economic stringency and that unnecessary ostentation will not be welcomed. But this is not new: when the Queen married Prince Philip in 1947, in the period of austerity soon after the war, the then young Princess Elizabeth used 300 clothing coupons to buy the material for the dress for her own big day, also in Westminster Abbey.

The Royal Family and Kate Middleton's parents will pay for the wedding and, despite any economic gloom, everyone will want to see an event full of the pageantry for which Britain is renowned, that can be enjoyed by the whole nation and globally.

The ring that William places on his bride's finger as they make their vows will be made of rare Welsh gold. All royal wedding rings made since 1923 have been fashioned from a single nugget given to the Royal Family for the Queen Mother's wedding.

If there is not enough of the original nugget left, the bands that the couple exchange will be made of gold from the same Snowdonian mines.

It is likely that William's younger brother Harry will be his 'supporter' (royal bridegrooms have supporters rather than best men), although there is a chance that one of William's good friends might be asked. Harry and William are close, having endured the loss of their mother together and served together in the armed forces. Harry was enthusiastic about William's choice of a bride: 'It means I get a sister, which I have always wanted.'

Above: The magnificent West Front of Westminster Abbey, where
Prince William and Kate Middleton will be married.

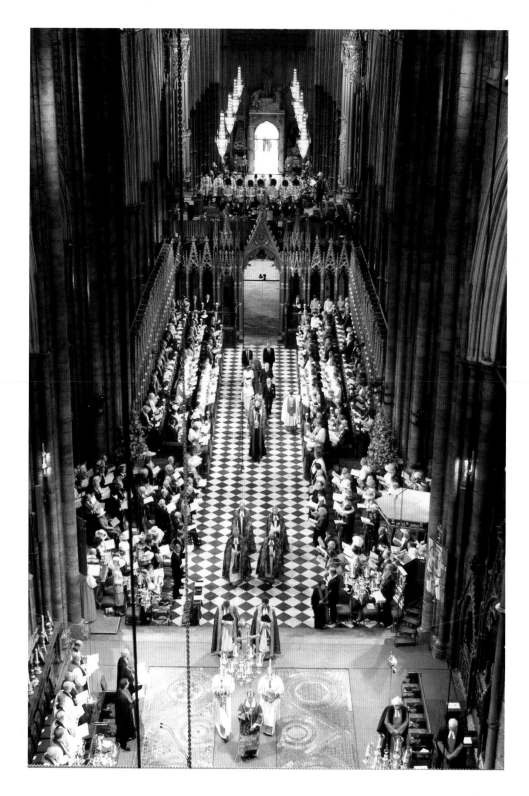

Above: Westminster Abbey is where the Royal Family commemorate special occasions. Here The Queen celebrates her Golden Jubilee. The picture shows the nave, quire and high altar from the West Door.

Westminster Abbey, built for Edward the Confessor and consecrated in December 1065, has been chosen for the royal wedding because of its great beauty.

Edward, who died a week after the consecration, was the first of 17 monarchs to be buried here, in January 1066. Less than a year later, on Christmas Day 1066, William the Conqueror became the first sovereign to be crowned in the great Abbey, beginning a virtually unbroken run of coronations up to that of the present Queen, almost 60 years ago.

It was in 1947 that this Gothic masterpiece, remodelled by Henry III in 1245, was the wedding venue for the young Princess Elizabeth's marriage to Lieutenant Philip Mountbatten, later the Duke of Edinburgh. She was following the example of her own mother, the then Elizabeth Bowes-Lyon, Duchess of York, who married Prince Albert at the high altar here in 1923. Prince Albert became King George VI when he succeeded to the throne. When the Queen Mother died in 2002 at the age of 101, her funeral was held here. Although William and Kate have chosen Westminster Abbey, it may reawaken sombre memories for William of his mother's funeral, 13 years ago, when he and his brother walked, heads bowed, behind her coffin.

The great stone walls and Gothic arches encompass hundreds of years of British history. At the west end of the Abbey's nave is the Tomb of the Unknown Warrior, a poignant symbol of the tragedy of war. Others buried or commemorated here include the poet Geoffrey Chaucer, Sir Isaac Newton, Samuel Johnson and Charles Darwin. The historic abbey – its full title the Collegiate Church of St Peter, Westminster – is what is known as a 'Royal Peculiar', belonging directly to the sovereign and standing at the centre of very many royal occasions.

When the betrothed couple announced their intention to make their marriage vows in Westminster Abbey, Prince William's private secretary, Jamie Lowther-Pinkerton, said that they were moved to choose the venue for its beauty, its 1,000-year-old royal history and its relative intimacy. In spite of its size, he explained, there was a feeling of 'intimate space' at the high altar, almost like that of a parish church.

'We know that the world will be watching on 29 April and the couple are very, very keen indeed that the spectacle should be a classic example of what Britain does best,' Mr Lowther-Pinkerton said.

The Dean of Westminster, the Very Reverend Dr John Hall, was delighted at Prince William and his bride-to-be's choice of wedding venue. 'We are very pleased that they have chosen Westminster Abbey for their marriage and look forward to the detailed planning for what will be a great and happy occasion for the couple themselves, for their families and friends, for the country and Commonwealth and for well-wishers across the globe,' he said.

Westminster Abbey is close to Buckingham Palace and the journey between the two follows a natural procession route through Trafalgar Square and Whitehall. Up to two million well-wishers are expected to turn out on the day to cheer the couple.

The usual visitor entrance to the Abbey is through the north door but wedding guests, including the Royal Family, will enter the Abbey, with its soaring arches and magnificent blue and gold interior, by way of the West Door between the distinctive, tall 18th-century Gothic twin towers.

This imposing entrance, taking guests directly into the nave, is flooded with light from the great West Window, which illuminates the whole building. Those who are able to look more closely will see that the stained glass depicts Abraham, Isaac and Jacob in the company of 14 prophets. Most guests will walk past the Tomb of the Unknown Warrior at the west end of the nave.

The bride, on her father's arm, will stand briefly in this light-filled space before the first notes of her entrance music ring out on the great organ, and she processes slowly up the nave and into the quire and sanctuary, followed by her attendants. The nave will seat many of the 2,000 guests, while the quire will hold not only guests, but also the Abbey choir.

Kate's father Michael Middleton will hand her into the safe-keeping of her husband-to-be, Prince William, who will be waiting for his bride near the high altar. William and his supporter (the royal name for a best man), will have

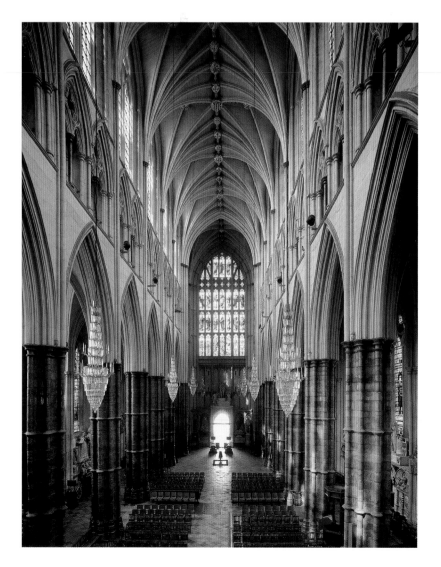

Left: Westminster Abbey nave, viewed from the quire screen and looking towards the West Door.

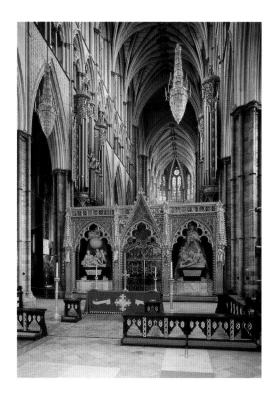

Kate Middleton, accompanied by her father Michael, will travel to Westminster Abbey in the style expected of a future queen. They will ride in the Glass Coach, one of the magnificent carriages kept in the Royal Mews and brought out only for ceremonial occasions.

Once Kate and her husband William have received congratulations and best wishes from all the guests as they make their joyful way back down the aisle, they will leave the Abbey in the equally historic open-topped 1902 State Landau.

entered the Abbey by way of the Poets' Corner door, by the Chapter House on the south side of the historic building. Kate will be on his left as they move forward to take their vows together.

As the couple stand before the high altar, they will see at their feet one of the Abbey's great treasures – the 13th-century Cosmati pavement, an intricate marble 'mosaic' design depicting a stationary earth at the centre of the universe.

Her Majesty the Queen and the Royal Family will sit in the south transept, the site of the famous Poets' Corner. Although in 1400 Geoffrey Chaucer was the first to be buried here, it was not for his wonderful *Canterbury Tales*, but because his day job was that of Clerk of Works to the Palace of Westminster. He was later joined by others including Edmund Spenser, Charles Dickens, Robert Browning and Rudyard Kipling.

The bride's own family will be seated in the north transept, where, sitting in the light cast from the beautiful Rose Window and surrounded by statues of British statesmen, including William Pitt, Sir Robert Peel, Gladstone and Disraeli, they will be able to watch their daughter's every response as she marries Prince William.

The star of any wedding is the bride – and her dress. The guests, the flowers, the cake, the coaches, even the thousand-carat power of sensational jewellery worn by the rich and famous from around the world, cannot compete with the bridal gown. It will be guarded with as much care as the bride herself and nothing will persuade its designer and those few in the know to reveal its secrets before the bride arrives at Westminster Abbey on 29 April.

This is not just any wedding dress. It is the gown worn by the future Queen. It must be sensational but classic, stunning but timeless. It will become a trendsetter, seen by billions around the world. It will make its designer a superstar.

Kate will choose a British designer to create her dress, and there is plenty of talent for her to explore. She may ask Stella McCartney, who made Madonna's dress, or she could be daring enough to commission the sometimes outrageous Vivienne Westwood to make her gown. There is Jenny Packham, Jasper Conran, Amanda Wakeley, John Galliano at Dior or the Welsh designer Julien Macdonald. Hotly tipped is Daniella 'Issa' Helayel, who has already made many dresses for the future Queen Catherine, including the sapphire blue silk-jersey wrap dress she wore when the engagement was announced in November.

Left: Members of the Royal Family wave from the balcony of Buckingham Palace after the wedding of Princess Elizabeth and Prince Philip in November 1947.

Below: Buckingham Palace, where crowds gather to celebrate great royal occasions.

And who will she choose to accompany her on that long walk down the nave of Westminster Abbey? Her sister Pippa, party-planner and girl-about-town, is an obvious choice and so, too, is Zara Phillips, Olympic horsewoman and daughter of the Princess Royal. Kate might choose her old school friend from Marlborough days, Alicia Fox-Pitt. Smaller bridesmaids could include Eloise, the young daughter of Lady Helen Taylor (daughter of the Duke of Kent) and the elder child of Prince Edward and Sophie Countess of Wessex, Lady Louise Windsor. Pages could include Prince William's godson, Konstantine Alexios, grandson of King Constantine of Greece, and young Viscount Severn, Prince Edward's son.

Traditionally a royal wedding has a guest list filled with crowned heads, statesmen, politicians and dignitaries from around the world. Prince William and Kate Middleton have made it clear that they will be very much in control of their big day and, while the great and the good will certainly take their places in the Abbey, many young friends of the couple will add a lively touch to the ceremony and reception.

The Royal Mint is producing a £5 coin to mark the engagement of Prince William and Kate Middleton – the first time in its long history that it has struck a commemorative coin for an engagement.

Left: The Glass Coach, in which the bride and her father will travel to Westminster Abbey.

Left: Prince William and his bride will leave Westminster Abbey in the open-topped 1902 State Landau.

FROM STUDENTS TO *Sweethearts*

K ate Middleton has waited a long time for her prince. The story of her romance with Prince William, from university days in Scotland, where they eventually shared a flat with friends, to gradual public appearances and cosy domesticity in out-of the-way cottages, is a slow-burning tale that has taken seven years to reach its denouement.

Kate and William went up to St Andrews University in September 2001. They were billeted in the same hall of residence, St Salvator's, and they were both studying Art History. William remembers those days: 'We were friends for over a year first and it just sort of blossomed. We just spent more time with each other, had a good giggle, lots of fun, and realized we shared the same interests and had a really good time,' he said.

Kate's memories of their first meeting are more personal: 'I actually think I went bright red and sort of scuttled off, feeling very shy,' she revealed.

There is no forgetting the Prince's reaction to Kate's appearance in the annual charity fashion show at a St Andrews hotel, during their second term at

Why did William wait so long to propose to the woman who is clearly the love of his life? He said that he knew the pressure of royal life was daunting and he wanted to give Kate the opportunity to see 'what happens on the other side'. 'I wanted to give her the chance to see and to back out if she needed to, before it all got too much,' he said.

Right: Kate was a guest at Prince William's graduation from Cranwell in April 2008, joining members of the Royal Family for the occasion.

Right: Kate caught Prince William's eye when she modelled in a student fashion show at St Andrews in March 2002.

Far right: Kate and William have a private conversation at Beaufort Polo Club in Gloucestershire in June 2005.

university. He paid £200 for a front row seat and was bowled over when Kate, who had become a friend, sashayed down the catwalk in a sheer shift dress. 'Wow!' was his reaction. 'Kate's hot!' he told a friend.

Although Kate might have welcomed his attention, she already had a boyfriend and did not want to give the wrong impression. She wisely kept the obvious attraction she and the young Prince were feeling for each other low key, and let matters develop slowly.

By the time they went up for their second year, they had become part of a group of four friends sharing a flat in the town, but still they managed to keep things discreet, never touching or holding hands in public, arriving at parties separately and, to the world and the sharp-eyed press, they were just good friends.

It was Kate who persuaded Prince William not to give up his university course when, in the early days, he decided that Art History was not for him. She was instrumental in ensuring that he carried on studying, later switching his degree to Geography.

By the time William's 21st birthday was celebrated with a party at Windsor Castle in June 2003, it is likely that William and Kate were romantically linked, although the Prince denied that he had a steady girlfriend.

After the Prince's proposal was accepted came the hardest part for the happy couple – keeping their good news secret for almost four weeks. Kate gave back the ring for safe keeping and, for a while she, her fiancé and her father, whose permission William had sought, were the only three people to know.

As friendship turned slowly to love, the many ways that the couple were well-suited became apparent.

William, the handsome young man who will one day be King, could have had his pick of European princesses and aristocratic young women for his bride. But his heart has been captured by an ordinary, although extraordinarily attractive, girl from the Home Counties.

This bodes well for the future, indicating that William is unpretentious and will listen to his own feelings rather than trying to satisfy convention.

In Kate he has found a woman with whom he feels comfortable. She is sporty and shares his love of the outdoor life – a must for anyone joining the Royal Family – and is cheerful, resourceful, uncomplicated and creative.

They share a sense of humour: 'She's got a really naughty sense of humour, which kind of helps me, because I've got a really dry sense of humour. We had a good laugh – and things happened,' he said.

They were close enough during their third and final years at university to share a secluded cottage, establishing a cosy domesticity, but still managing to keep the relationship a secret. Their tight circle of friends helped, never breaking the code of silence that bound them to the young couple.

But once they left university that was impossible. William had to fulfil his royal duties and forge his career, the press never far away. By the time the pair had been spotted on the slopes enjoying a skiing holiday together at Klosters, Switzerland, the secret was out in the open. No one had seen them behaving like lovers, but they were often spotted together and suddenly, Kate – who had just moved into a flat in central London with an old friend from her boarding-school days – found the full glare of the media spotlight on her private life.

She coped admirably, resigned to the fact that she would have to dress carefully, wear make-up and be suitably coiffured every time she stepped outside in order to face the photographers lying in wait.

Kate kept a low profile at major events. She was not seen at the marriage of Prince Charles and Camilla Parker Bowles in 2005, although she did attend other weddings with William that year.

Left: Prince William takes part in the Sovereign's Parade at Sandhurst, in December 2006, as he passes out to receive his commission with the Household Cavalry in the Blues and Royals.

Since 2007 Kate has appeared at a number of high-profile events, including the Princes' Concert for Diana, where she was a VIP guest in the royal box, and William's 'Wings' presentation ceremony in April 2008. She was also invited to the wedding of Peter Phillips, The Queen's grandson. This was the occasion where she first met The Queen. And in June 2008 she was asked to St George's Chapel, Windsor Castle, where she watched William's investiture into the Order of the Garter.

Above: Kate Middleton, flanked by her father Michael and mother Carole, is an invited guest at Prince William's passing out parade at The Royal Military Academy, Sandhurst.

Far left: William is a keen polo player and here Kate is at the Ham Polo Club in Surrey to watch him play.

Left: William and Kate on the way home after partying at London nightclub Boujis, in January 2007.

Although William continued to deny that marriage was in the air, their relationship was widely accepted, especially after he was photographed kissing Kate at another Klosters holiday in 2006. It seemed too that the Royal Family had accepted her as William's girlfriend when images of William and his father, happy and at ease in her company, were widely circulated in the press.

Pressure from William's life in the forces was blamed for the couple's brief separation in early spring 2007 – but within weeks they were back together again as if nothing had happened.

A TWENTY-FIRST-CENTURY *Prince*

Early in the morning of 23 June 1982, a young father stood proudly on the steps outside St Mary's Hospital, Paddington, tenderly holding his newborn baby son.

He was not allowed to leave quietly. Cameras flashed and whirred, while journalists and television crews shouted questions as Prince Charles, heir to the throne, held the child who would also one day be King.

But the then unnamed baby, just 36-hours old, who bore a tag on his tiny wrist identifying him only as 'Baby Wales', scarcely stirred, undisturbed by the commotion and public rejoicing at his arrival.

'The birth of our son has given us both more pleasure than you can imagine,' said a tired and delighted Prince. 'It has made me incredibly proud and somewhat amazed.'

Prince William Arthur Philip Louis of Wales entered the world at 9.03pm on 21 June in the private Lindo Wing of the hospital. He was driven home to Kensington Palace, where he was to spend the next 16 years of his life.

William's great-grandmother, the late Queen Elizabeth, the Queen Mother, celebrated her birthday on 4 August and that was the date in 1982 chosen for the christening of the newest member of the Royal Family. The ceremony, in the Music Room at Buckingham Palace, was conducted by the then Archbishop of Canterbury, Dr Robert Runcie. Young William was dressed in the Royal Family's ancient Honiton lace christening gown, first worn by the future King Edward VII. The two-month old baby was baptized with water from the River Jordan, poured into the traditional Lily Font, used for every royal christening since 1840.

Left: Young William after his first day at nursery school, with a finger puppet he had made for his mother.

Prince William became the first 'heir presumptive' (an heir, other than the first in line to the throne) to be born in an ordinary hospital, albeit in an expensive private wing, rather than in a royal residence. This was seen by many as a sign that the young Prince was entering a changing world, far different from that occupied by his father in 1948.

Right: Prince William at the age of 19.

William's mother, Princess Diana, whose love for her children shone through all she did, was determined to be hands-on when it came to bringing up her children. From the start, she gave William the constant attention and affection all babies need. It was she who nicknamed him 'Wills' and, later 'Wombat', two names that have stayed with him. Her first big test came just a few weeks after his birth when she and Prince Charles were due to leave Britain for a long tour of Australia. Those who assumed that Diana would leave her precious son behind, in the care of his nanny and the nursery staff, were more than surprised when the young mother insisted that her child should travel with her.

If traditionalists criticized her 'modern' approach to rearing the heir presumptive, the rest of the world did not. There was general approval as pictures were shown of William's nanny, Barbara Barnes, carrying the baby from the aircraft onto Australian soil as they landed on the other side of the world.

There was a surge of excitement outside a small private nursery school in Notting Hill Gate as the children arrived for the new term in September 1985. A crowd of reporters and photographers jostled for position, cameras trained on one small boy dressed in red shorts and a red check shirt.

It had been no easy decision to send William to nursery school: royal children were normally taught at home by a governess until they were at least seven years old. However Diana was keen that her son should escape the hothouse atmosphere of the Palace and learn how to socialize with other children.

The transition from being the centre of attention of his nanny, Barbara Barnes, to one of many children at school was probably a hard lesson to learn, but it has stood William in good stead.

Just two years later he moved from nursery school to the pre-prep Wetherby, West London, where there was more scope for his obvious aptitude for sport and enjoyment in taking part in school activities. It was at this time that a new nanny, Ruth Wallace, arrived at Kensington Palace to teach her young charge not only self-reliance but also the importance of consideration and kindness to others.

Both William and, later, his younger brother Harry moved on to become boarders at Ludgrove School in Berkshire, where William excelled at sport. He was tall for his age and soon became captain of both the rugby and hockey teams, and one of the school stars at clay pigeon shooting, having learnt how to handle a gun from a very early age. Another early lesson that every member of the Royal Family has to learn is that they are forever in the public eye. As eventual heir to the throne, William has had to understand that the job is one for life. During his childhood and as he grew up he accompanied his parents on a number of official duties so that he could get used to the attention he will always receive.

He has inherited not only the Windsor sense of duty, but also his mother's easy manner with the crowds, and his own charisma and self-assurance stands him in good stead in all his public duties.

Above: Princes William and Harry and their cousin, Peter Phillips, play on a fire engine on the Sandringham Estate in Norfolk, in January 1988. The princes' mother, Princess Diana, is watching over them.

Above: William takes part in a race at a school sports day, in June 1988.

One of those first public engagements happened when, just eight years old, he accompanied his parents on a visit to Llandaff Cathedral in 1991 to celebrate St David's Day. A visit to the principality from which William takes his title was an appropriate baptism into public life and he wore a bright yellow daffodil in his buttonhole. It was when the young Prince, under the watchful eye of his mother, signed his name in the visitors' book at the cathedral, that onlookers noticed that he was left-handed.

Far left: The Princess of Wales, holding Prince Harry by the hand and with William at her side, arrives at the Nottingham Medical Centre in September 1990, to visit Prince Charles, who was a patient at the hospital.

Left: William, wearing a daffodil, accompanies his parents on an official visit to Wales in 1991.

Below: William and Harry enjoy a boat trip with their mother, Princess Diana, at Niagara Falls in 1991.

For several years Princess Diana was the unofficial mascot of the Welsh rugby team and a fervent supporter, taking William and Harry with her to international matches. Both boys took pride in learning the words of the Welsh National anthem – in Welsh – so that they could join in the community singing.

Another break with royal tradition came when it was time for the young Prince to continue his education. The sometimes tough regime of Gordonstoun, the Scottish public school attended by William's grandfather, father and uncles, was eschewed in favour of Eton College, possibly the most famous educational establishment in the world. The Berkshire college, with its centuries-long tradition of producing self-confident young men, was a happy selection. It was the first choice of both Diana and the Queen Mother, while William was pleased, not only that many of his friends from Ludgrove would be with him, but also that the school was close to Windsor Castle where he could join his grandmother, The Queen, for Sunday tea.

'William Wales' signed the Eton schoolbook in September 1995, on his first day there. His study-bedroom, in Manor House (where he was the only boy afforded the luxury of a private bathroom) was a cell-like 4 metres (13 feet) by 3 metres (10 feet) with a narrow single bed. William stamped his own mark on it by putting up a picture of Aston Villa football team, a signed poster of All Saints (his favourite band) and various pin-up posters.

As at Ludgrove, William excelled at sports, enjoying football, rugby, and shone especially in the school pool where he became the 'Keeper of Swimming' – Eton-speak for captain of the swimming team.

He did well academically too, gaining three A-levels with grades good enough to win a place at St Andrews University. But first he decided to see something of the world by taking a gap year.

Travel, adventure and education were the criteria for the widening of William's education. His first destination was Belize, the former British Honduras in Central America, where he joined the Welsh Guards on exercise in the wet, stifling hot and humid jungle. He had to learn what to do if bitten by a snake (chop its head off and keep the body to assess the dose of venom received), and how to kill and gut chickens before cooking them over an open fire. It was here that he first used semi-automatic weapons.

Far left: Prince William during his first year at Eton.

Left: Prince William captains his team in a school football tournament between Eton houses Gaileys (the Prince's team) and Hursts.

Below: William wearing his patriotic 'Pop' waistcoat, a privilege of sixth formers at Eton.

Right: On his gap year in Chile, the Prince, against the backdrop of the Andes, walks to work in the village of Tortel.

The distinctive Eton uniform of black tail coat, striped trousers, waistcoat and white bow tie was established in 1820, when the whole establishment went into mourning for the death of King George III. When William was elected a member of 'Pop', the elite group of sixth formers at the college allowed to wear waistcoats of their own choice – the more startling the better – he enthusiastically took advantage of this privilege.

If the jungles of Belize were steamy and uncomfortable, the soft white sands, blue sea, warm sun and gentle breezes of Mauritius in the Indian Ocean were pure delight. One 'Brian Woods', aka William of Wales, registered on the island of Rodrigues here, as a helper with the Royal Geographical Society's 'Shoals of Capricorn' programme on marine conservation.

Chile came next, during the cold, wet and miserable rainy season. The first week of this Raleigh International expedition saw torrential rain day and night. The young volunteers, soaked to the skin, had never experienced anything like it.

'Eventually even the tent became wet through; it was saturated ... we became quite demoralized even though we somehow managed to keep ourselves going by singing, telling jokes and stores ...,' said William on his return. But, when the rain stopped, the volunteers moved to the village of Tortel, teaching English to the children and making friends with the locals.

Anyone seeing the two young sons of Diana, Princess of Wales walking slowly, heads bowed, behind her funeral cortège on 6 September 1997 could not have failed to be moved. The boys were at particularly vulnerable ages – William was 15 and his brother Harry just two years younger – when their beloved mother died in a tragic car accident in Paris.

Despite the public outpouring of grief, the young princes, whatever they were certainly feeling inwardly, kept their emotions firmly under control, showing a maturity that belied their years.

William took on the mantle of older brother with particular care after Diana's death, giving the younger Harry the unqualified support that he may have needed.

The boys have found security at their father's home Highgrove, Gloucestershire, with Prince Charles who has coped admirably with their care since Princess Diana's death. The family circle now includes the Duchess of Cornwall, the former Camilla Parker Bowles, Charles's long-time companion and second wife.

Since William went away to school, first to Ludgrove and then to Eton, his domestic life has been one of contrasts. At home – Highgrove, St James's Palace in London, Balmoral in Scotland or Sandringham in Norfolk – he would be gently woken each morning by a footman bearing a 'calling tray' with his pot of coffee and biscuits. His curtains would be drawn, the radio turned on and clothes laid out by a valet, primed the night before of that day's activities. Breakfast included a 'full English' or a choice of cereals and fruit. William usually ate the latter.

Prince William, who changed his university subject from Art History to Geography won a Scottish Master of Arts degree with upper second class honours – the highest university honours gained by an heir to the British throne.

Left: William, Harry and their father, Prince Charles, became a close-knit trio after the death of Princess Diana in August 1997.

Right: Prince Charles and his sons enjoy a skiing holiday in the Swiss resort Klosters in 2005.

There was no such luxury at Eton and there were certainly no servants to make the early morning routine go smoothly when, in September 2001, William Wales went up to St Andrews University in Scotland, joining the 6,000 other students who swell the population of the town during term time.

At first he lived in the rambling Gothic co-educational hall of residence, St Salvator's Hall ('Sallies' to its inhabitants), where he tumbled out of bed in the morning, showered and helped himself to breakfast in the communal dining hall, sitting next to whoever happened to be there at the time. He usually opted for the healthy choice but just occasionally fell prey to a couple of bacon butties and a mug of tea.

Breakfast over and teeth brushed, he would join fellow students in the lecture rooms or see his tutor to discuss an essay or, if there was no work on the agenda, would stroll into town to buy the newspapers and perhaps join friends for a coffee.

It was at St Andrews that William met Kate Middleton with whom he and two other friends eventually moved out of hall to share a flat.

William's grandmother, Her Majesty Queen Elizabeth II, laid down a few ground rules for William at university. These were: no smoking, only moderate drinking and certainly no drugs. If he dated a woman he was never to be seen kissing her in public. Nor was he ever to ask his bodyguard to leave him alone, even at private parties. The last was a rule that William had observed since he was old enough to understand the ways of the world: never to discuss any member of the Royal Family, even with those to whom he had become close.

On Remembrance Sunday 2010, just two days before the announcement of his engagement to Kate Middleton and the media frenzy that the news provoked, William decided to pay his respects to the British troops risking their lives in Afghanistan. To the surprise of many he flew out to join the men and women in the front line, taking part in the Remembrance Day Service with them.

The future King has a strong sense of duty, instilled in him by his Windsor forebears. He also takes a keen interest in various charitable causes, many of them once supported by his mother Princess Diana. He and his brother Harry had been taken by their mother on visits to Centrepoint, the charity for young homeless people supported by Diana and also to shelters and clinics for those suffering from HIV AIDS. He took on patronage of Centrepoint, and to prove his commitment William went so far as to sleep rough on a freezing December night near Blackfriars Bridge.

He and Harry helped raise £40,000 for survivors of the devastating Asian tsunami by playing in a charity polo match just days after the terrible event on Boxing Day 2004. A week later the brothers volunteered at a British Red Cross distribution centre, making up aid packages for those affected by the disaster.

Above: William shakes hands with the crowd at the BAFTA awards at the Royal Opera House, Covent Garden, in February 2010.

Above: Prince William visits HM Naval Base at Faslane, in Scotland, to present gold pins to submariners in October 2010.

Right: William and his brother Harry went together to Africa in June 2010 where William joined a game of football with these boys in Semonkong, Lesotho.

Even at the age of 15, Prince William was aware of his mother's passion for charity work. He was pleased that the 2,000-strong congregation who attended her funeral service in Westminster Abbey had included representatives of the many organizations that she had helped and supported.

While on his gap year William clearly enjoyed working with young children in the southern Chilean village of Tortel, where he taught English at the school and helped with various building projects. Back in the UK he did a stint of work experience at the children's unit at the Royal Marsden Hospital and soon became a patron of the institution. He is also a patron of Mountain Rescue England and Wales and of the African-based Tusk Trust which works to conserve wildlife, and help with community development and education across the vast continent. His first official duty with the charity was in 2007, when he launched a 5,000 mile (8,000km) bike ride across Africa.

Sport is high on Prince William's agenda and it follows that he has become the figurehead of some sporting organizations, raising money for charity through activities such as polo. He has taken part in charity runs with teams from Sandhurst and Clarence House to boost the coffers of Sports Relief, and he is also patron of the English Schools' Swimming Association.

Since he was a schoolboy William has supported Aston Villa football team, and in May 2006 he became President of England's Football Association. His grandmother, The Queen, is patron of the Welsh Rugby Union and the Prince is in effect her deputy, having been appointed vice royal patron of the Union.

Sometime in the future Prince William of Wales KG FRS will be crowned King William V. This is his destiny and every aspect of his life has been shaped with his role as sovereign the predominant factor.

With the kingship in prospect, William can never be too ambitious about a career or profession, nor will he ever know the struggle of having to make his own way in life. What he can do while he waits, as his father has done for several decades, is to further his military career and to become accustomed to the round of public duties and sponsorship of a variety of causes.

After leaving university William underwent work experience from land management to banking, but, in the best royal tradition, eventually settled on a career in the armed forces.

He graduated from Sandhurst in December 2006 after spending almost a year at the Royal Military Academy there, receiving his commission as a lieutenant and watched at the passing out parade by his proud father and his grandmother The Queen.

Left: Prince William, President of the English Football Association, is seen here with David Beckham and Prince Harry at a reception to mark the 2010 FIFA World Cup in June 2010, in Johannesburg.

Below: On his first official visit overseas, in January 2010, William toured New Zealand and Australia on behalf of The Queen. Here he meets well-wishers after spending time at the children's ward at Wellington Regional Hospital, New Zealand.

During his secondment to RAF Cranwell, the Prince was part of the crew on a C-17 Globemaster sent to Afghanistan to bring back the body of a British serviceman, who had been killed in action. William was known affectionately by his fellow airmen as 'Billy the Fish'.

'The one thing his father and I were absolutely agreed on was that William would have as normal an upbringing as possible,' said his mother Diana Princess of Wales. But normality is difficult to achieve for a young man who is unable to make a move without informing his bodyguards and on whom the hopes of the monarchy are fixed. What William has done, probably more than any other member of the Royal Family, is to bridge the gap between the monarchy and the British people. His marriage to Kate Middleton will strengthen that bridge.

Right: On Remembrance Day in 2010 William paid a surprise visit to troops in Afghanistan and laid a memorial wreath.

Lieutenant William Wales followed his younger brother Harry into the Blues and Royals (the Household Cavalry Regiment) as a troop commander in an armoured reconnaissance unit.

His wish to see active service was discouraged, so William trained in both the Royal Navy and the Royal Air Force, winning commissions as sub-lieutenant in the former and flying officer in the latter.

An intensive four-month training course at Cranwell won him his RAF wings, presented to him in April 2008 by his father, a ceremony that was watched by, among others, his bride-to-be.

A period with the Royal Navy followed, during which William, on board HMS *Iron Duke* in the Caribbean, took part in a secret underwater mission, helping to foil drug smugglers.

Although William has been denied military service in combat zones, he was still able to be an active member of the armed services and, with this as the aim, he trained to become a helicopter pilot with the RAF's Search and Rescue Force.

He is now based at RAF Valley on Anglesey, where he is expected to remain with No. 22 Squadron until 2013, working aboard Sea King helicopters. His first rescue mission, as co-pilot in October 2010, was to an offshore gas rig in Morecambe Bay to airlift a sick man to hospital on the mainland.

A MODERN
Princess

Kate Middleton, our future Queen Catherine, knows that when she marries Prince William she is, in a way, marrying the whole nation. When he succeeds to the throne her husband will be subjected to an almost daily round of public duties, and she will be at his side.

Having been close to William for seven years, Kate must have some idea of the constant pressure they will both be under. William certainly does: on the day of their engagement he told the world that he had waited so long to ask her to be his wife in order to give her the chance to 'back out' of such an enormous commitment.

Kate is, in royal parlance, 'a commoner', a middle-class woman from a wealthy self-made family with loving parents who have given her every advantage educationally and socially. She is well-mannered without being stuffy, charming without being precious, good-tempered and accommodating but with a will and mind of her own that will endear her to the British public.

Kate's parents and siblings have already passed the 'loyalty test'. In the years that she and William have been together they have never let slip any details about the relationship. And, because she has had to behave as discreetly as a royal, her own family, especially her mother Carole and sister Pippa, have been an ever-present comfort, always ready with dependable support and advice.

Catherine Elizabeth Middleton was born at the Royal Berkshire Hospital, Reading on 9 January 1982, making her just five months older than her fiancé.

On her mother's side Kate is descended from a line of Durham miners. Her maternal grandfather, Ron Goldsmith, left school at 14 and eventually established a building business in Southall, West London. His daughter Carole, Kate's mother, joined BOAC, the then international airline, as a stewardess and, during the 1970s, met and married Michael Middleton.

Mr Middleton had grown up in Leeds where his father, a pilot, came from forebears who were solicitors, mill owners and minor landowners. Michael, for a while a steward with BOAC, trained as a pilot before working in airline administration.

Christened 'Catherine' but known to the British public as 'Kate', Prince William's future bride has indicated that she will use the more formal version of her name when she marries. On her husband's eventual succession to the throne she will become the sixth Queen Catherine, following Henry V's wife Catherine of Valois (d. 1437), three wives of Henry VIII, Catherine of Aragon (d. 1536), Catherine Howard (beheaded 1542) and Catherine Parr (d. 1548), and later, Catherine of Braganza who married Charles II in 1662.

It was after the birth of their third child James that Carole Middleton had the brainwave that would make the family fortune. She spotted a gap in the party market and set up a mail-order business selling costumes, toys, games and novelties for parties of all sorts.

By the time the business had expanded successfully, adapting well to the advent of the Internet, the Middletons – Carole and Michael with their three children Kate, Pippa and James – were able to move into their large five-bedroom detached family house in the Berkshire village of Buckleberry.

Above: Kate Middleton, hailed as a charming and sensible young woman, seen here at a game fair at Blenheim Palace in 2004.

The success of the Middleton's family business, now run from a large barn at their Berkshire home, enabled Kate's parents to give her a privileged education, sending her first to St Andrew's School in Pangbourne and then to Marlborough College, where she justified the £29,000 a year fees by becoming an admirable student academically, socially and on the sports field.

Marlborough College, founded in 1843 by the Church of England for the sons of impoverished clergy, is built around a pretty Queen Anne house on rolling Wiltshire downland and has turned out some of Britain's most prominent women. Prime Minister's wife Samantha Cameron and Sally Bercow, wife of the Speaker of the House of Commons, were educated there, as were Princess Eugenie of York, Emily Sheffield (deputy editor of *Vogue*), writers Frances Osborne and Lauren Child, (creator of the Charlie and Lola books), model Stella Tennant and designer Antonia Robinson.

Friends who were at school with Kate remember her as an initially shy girl who transformed into a confident outgoing teenager, hard-working, athletic and easy-going. She was described as popular, level-headed and talented. At Marlborough she met the children of the rich and famous but like all Marlburiennes, she learnt how to be fair

Poet John Betjeman was a pupil at Marlborough College and loathed it – 'Doom, Shivering doom! Inexorable bells to early school,' he wrote. Maybe he would have liked it better if girls, who were first admitted to the sixth form in 1968, had been there in his day.

Above: Kate, centre, as a young pupil at St Andrew's Prep School in Pangbourne, Berkshire.

Right: Kate arrives to see Prince William graduate at St Andrews University, in June 2005.

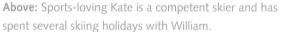

Above: Sports-loving Kate is a competent skier and has spent several skiing holidays with William.

Above: Kate, complete with Indiana Jones-style hat, shops for socks at the Gatcombe Park Festival in 2005.

and tough. Marlborough girls have the reputation of being polite without being bland, thoughtful with appearing too earnest, and thoroughly civilized.

Kate, who achieved three good A-levels, including A grades for Maths and Art, discovered that you could not be a shrinking violet or take yourself too seriously at the college. But she did find the freedom to discover herself and not worry about what others might think. The girls were not expected to be brilliant, but they had to join in. Many of her fellow pupils were unconventional but most were passionate about something, whether it was writing, painting, history, science or music.

Kate became head of her house, Elmhurst, where she is still remembered as being very good at mucking in, playing games – she was captain of the school hockey team – and acting. She was also known for her dependability and loyalty; all the qualities, in fact, for a perfect modern princess.

Like her husband-to-be, Kate opted for a gap year before going on to St Andrews University to study Art History. And, like William, she spent time working on a project in Chile, also visiting the Caribbean and Florence.

By the time Kate arrived at Marlborough, once a boys-only college, girls were a fixture, but when the first female students were admitted in 1968 the prospect of being watched and 'marked' by dozens of boys was a daunting one. But it was character-forming. 'Anything after walking across court for the first time, watched by all those boys, is a piece of cake,' said one former pupil.

When Kate Middleton went up to St Andrews University in the small Scottish town of the same name, she was not the only pupil there from her school, Marlborough College. Some of her former schoolmates knew Prince William, so it was not long before he and Kate were on friendly terms – although she admits she felt embarrassed when they were first introduced.

But that embarrassment was quickly overcome. By the end of freshers' week Kate had been dubbed the prettiest girl at 'Sallies' (St Salvator's Hall) and both she and the Prince were enrolled on the same course. Soon they were meeting over the breakfast muesli and fruit, served in the grand ground-floor dining hall with the light filtering through its stained-glass windows, portraits of Scottish philosophers lined up above them on the walls.

They had a love of the countryside, sporting pursuits and swimming in common. By coincidence their gap years had followed a similar pattern and Kate was able to talk about the Renaissance art she had seen in Florence and which would be figuring on the Art History course.

But talking was all that happened at this stage. They both had romantic liaisons with other people during their first term and when William discovered that he was not enjoying his course, finding the workload challenging, there was serious talking to be done. A decision to switch to a Geography degree course and a growing interest in the pretty chestnut-haired student, who seemed quieter and more sympathetic than many of the others, did the trick.

At the beginning of their second year William and Kate, with two other friends, moved into a property in Hope Street in St Andrews town centre. This was fitted out like no other student accommodation, with bullet-proof windows, bomb-proof doors and a sophisticated laser security system. Here they entertained friends, threw dinner parties and allowed their romance to blossom.

Through all this, Kate was discretion itself. She was careful not to be seen in any compromising situation with William and it was not until they were photographed making their way together up the slopes on a ski lift at Klosters, in June 2004, that anyone outside their close-knit circle of friends had any inkling that they were romantically linked.

University friends remember that although Kate had become the girlfriend of the most eligible man at university, she never boasted or gloated. And, most importantly, she always followed the unwavering royal rule of never talking about their relationship.

St Andrews has a reputation as a university for forging long-lasting relationships. At William and Kate's graduation ceremony in June 2005, the university's vice-chancellor Dr Brian Lang uttered words that many have seen as prophetic: 'You will have made lifelong friends,' he told the young people seated in front of him. 'You may have met your husband or wife. Our title as the top match-making university in Britain signifies so much that is good about St Andrews, so we rely on you to go forth and multiply.'

Right: Kate and her sister Philippa watch Prince William play polo in June 2006.

Far right: Kate does a spot of shopping on the King's Road, London.

Right: Philippa joins her sister Kate at a book launch party in London.

Far right: In August 2007, Kate trained to join the crew of a traditional Chinese dragon boat, about to make a charity row across the English Channel.

Kate graduated from St Andrews University with a good degree in Art History, but she decided to make a career in the fashion business, for a while becoming an accessories buyer for the high street clothes chain Jigsaw.

But her parents' successful family company, selling partyware of all kinds, needed a marketing manager, so in 2007 she decided to work at promoting the business back home in rural Berkshire.

That all had to stop when she became William's fiancée. She had to hand over projects such as designing the Christmas catalogue, arranging press coverage for the thriving company, organizing photo shoots and visiting trade fairs to others; suddenly her job now was to become a member of the Royal Family.

Many royal marriages are arranged to unite two nations, or as a marriage of convenience between two families eager to strengthen their ties by such a union. This marriage is different. Kate and William are the prime movers and it is they who have made the decisions on their own terms calmly and soberly. It is clear that they are marrying for love, and with a great deal of friendship and goodwill on both sides.

Kate comes from a warm and happy family who have welcomed Prince William into their home without fuss or pretension, never boasting to the neighbours or letting slip details about the relationship to the media. That discretion, and Kate's own loyalty and quiet perseverance, has stood her in good stead, winning the approval of her future grandmother-in-law, The Queen.

Far left: Dressed for fun and games, Kate arrives at the Day-Glo Midnight Roller Disco in London in September 2008.

Left: A chic outfit for the wedding of Hugh van Cutsem to Rose Astor, at Burford in June 2005.

Above: Kate wears a traditional tweed suit and fashionably large sunglasses at the Cheltenham Gold Cup, in March 2007.

Above: Kate (centre) steps out in a summery outfit for the July 2010 wedding of Lady Rose Windsor and George Gilman at The Queen's Chapel, London.

Kate has been discreet, too, about past relationships. We know that in her first term at university she dated Rupert Finch, a talented cricketer and now a lawyer, but neither he nor she has ever spoken about their friendship.

Like William she enjoys partying but, even during their brief break-up in 2007, her name has never been linked to that of any other serious boyfriend.

Patience is another virtue and Kate has displayed that quality over the years when she and William have been playing the waiting game. During the many times that William has been away on royal duties, family holidays or undergoing his periods of training and service with the armed forces, Kate showed that she was prepared to stay at home without fuss and with the stoicism she will need to display for the rest of her life.

These qualities – her innate sense of discretion, the self-containment she has displayed throughout the relationship, and her good-humoured patience and resilience – have been noted by her future in-laws, who have clearly given Kate the royal seal of approval.

KATE'S *Style*

Prince William could not help but notice when 'quiet Kate', the girl he had enjoyed chatting to at breakfast in the university dining hall, sashayed down the catwalk wearing a sheer shift that did nothing to hide her black undergarments. But this revealing outfit, worn for a charity fashion show, is not Kate's normal style.

At university she was happy to wear the student 'uniform' of jeans, sweaters and jackets – the warmer the better, to cope with the bracing Scottish climate.

Kate is tall and slim, with long, glossy, deep-chestnut hair which she likes to wear loose and which suits her that way.

So she has adopted a refreshingly natural look which has won her several fashion accolades, including a listing in the top ten *Tatler* style icons, the 'most promising newcomer' award in a *Daily Telegraph* list of style winners and a place in *Vanity Fair*'s international best-dressed list.

Kate knows she has a lot to live up to: William's mother, the late Princess Diana, was an international style icon. But the great strength of the girl from the Home Counties is that she wears fashion in the same way as other women of her age, but with the advantage of long legs, a slender frame and a casual manner that belies any effort she might have made. Kate is a girl-next-door fashion icon that everyone can relate to.

Copies of Kate's sophisticated sapphire blue silk-jersey wrap dress, the hem falling just above the knee, with its long sleeves, plunging neckline and snug waist, sold out in hours after the announcement of the engagement. Up-market London boutiques and fashion stores had to reorder the £399 Issa dress after those already in stock flew out of the shops.

Right: Kate at the wedding of William's close friend Nicholas van Cutsem to Alice Hadden-Paton at The Guards Chapel, Wellington Barracks, London, in August 2009.

Her post-university style of jeans or casual trousers tucked into long leather boots and teamed with a blouse and jacket looked good. For the short while that she worked for high street fashion house Jigsaw she was to be spotted wearing their clothes, along with other stylish brands such as L.K. Bennett, Kew and Whistles.

But latterly her tastes have become more up-market and sophisticated. She is clearly supporting British fashion designers and brands, which is good news for the home-grown fashion market for whom she will become an ambassador. The brilliant-blue silk-jersey wrap dress that she wore to announce her engagement and that suited her so well is by Issa – a British company owned and run by Daniella Issa Helayel, now one of Kate's favourite designers.

Kate goes for clear, bright colours that display her dark good looks to perfection. Reds, deep pinks, and classic navy all look good on the royal bride-to-be, tailored into clinging dresses, scoop neck blouses and tops, and well-cut trousers that show off her slim figure. Tailored jackets, nipped in to her waist, are a favourite, teamed with casual trousers, scarves and hats for a chic city-girl-about-town look.

SHARING A *Life*

After the honeymoon comes the whole of the rest of their life together. Like many young couples, reluctant to enter the commitment of marriage without thoroughly testing the stresses and strains first, William and Kate have come through the fire and storm, their relationship proving fireproof and watertight. The pressure on these two must, at times, have been almost unbearable. William, brought up to be aware of the constant floodlight directed at his family, has, from very early days, been trained to cope, not to show emotion and to keep a buttoned stiff upper lip.

It is Kate who has given an excellent example of discretion and clear-headedness under extreme pressure. While she has waited for eight years for William to make a firm commitment, she has served her apprenticeship for her new job as wife of the future King – and she has passed that apprenticeship with star grades.

Despite sometimes unpleasant press jibes at her status as a middle-class girl with modest antecedents, and despite the loneliness she must have felt during their brief separation and the private agony of never being able to explain or justify, she has shown a toughness and remarkable forbearance and composure. Never once has she given an interview, or spoken to any member of the press. Her warm and well-modulated tones came as a surprise to many at the press gathering when the engagement was announced – it was the first time most had heard her speak. Kate, never without a wide attractive smile, her dark good looks framed by perfect glossy hair, charmed the assembled media as she radiated the happiness of a woman in love.

William, too, shows a love that has passed its long testing. It is a measure of the steps that he has taken to protect their privacy that we know very few personal details about their relationship. Their close-knit circle of friends have been, and will continue to be, extremely loyal through the first years of their married life.

The Prince and Kate Middleton have enjoyed exotic holidays in sun-drenched spots, from villas in Mustique to the beautiful wilderness of Kenya, where Prince William – with the sapphire ring that once belonged to his mother smuggled out of its safe and into his rucksack – made his proposal of marriage. They have enjoyed skiing holidays together and have spent weekends in cosy cottages, snuggled in front of the television. They have also had leisure time in houses owned by William's family, including Birkhall, Prince Charles's luxury hunting lodge on the Balmoral estate, where the Prince of Wales and the Duchess of Cornwall stayed after their own wedding. The honeymoon destination is anybody's guess, although the couple might just be tempted to revisit the wooden lodge on the slopes of Mount Kenya where William made his 'very romantic and very personal' proposal.

Above: William and Kate have been photographed at many of their friends' weddings. Now it is their turn to enjoy a happy married life.

Kate and William both know what lies ahead and it is already clear they will take their positions as King-in-Waiting and his Consort seriously. Their London life will be based in an official residence, almost certainly an apartment in Kensington Palace, where members of the British Royal Family have lived since Kensington was a village and where William and his brother Harry were brought up. The Duke and Duchess of Gloucester, the Duke and Duchess of Kent, and Prince and Princess Michael of Kent all have apartments here.

But family life will still be important to both William and Kate. He is probably the first senior member of the Royal Family to have spent time with ordinary people in a way that those of his father's generation could not, and he has shown himself to be able to relax with his peers, enjoying the company of those around him.

Part of Kate's attraction is her close and loving family; the Prince is comfortable with her parents, and has spent a considerable amount of time at their home, clearly enjoying their warmth and happiness. Kate's younger sister Philippa and brother James are part of the family circle, and the newly-weds will continue to be welcome as visitors after the wedding.

The long years they have been together have given them the chance to get to know each other's families, and it is clear that William's father and grandmother know that this union between middle England and a monarchy striving to be more modern is an excellent one. It is obvious that Kate is intelligent, good-looking, kind and down-

Left: As William continues to enjoying taking part in sport, including polo, Kate, as his wife, will turn out to watch him play.

Above: Kate enjoys leisure time with William and his family.

Right: Harry, William and Kate cheer the England rugby team at Twickenham.

It has been reported that a house will be built for the couple in Herefordshire, at Harewood Park, an estate belonging to the Duchy of Cornwall. Harewood Park is just an hour's drive from Highgrove, the Prince of Wales's home in Gloucestershire.

Almost as soon as the engagement was announced, organizations eager for an official visit from Prince William and Kate Middleton have been petitioning St James's Palace. But, although he will carry out some duties connected with those organizations of which he is already a patron, the Prince has no plans to increase the workload.

to-earth and it seems likely, coming as she does from a happy home, that she will create a similar setting for herself and William and for the children that they have said they hope to have.

Meanwhile William and Kate have a lot to share. They laugh together, teasing each other gently. Both are extremely good at all sorts of sport, from skiing to playing hockey, and both share a love of outdoor life. They have a circle of good friends in whose company they know they can relax and enjoy a normal social life. Kate is clearly happy to defer to William and it seems likely that she will devote her life to supporting him. He will be equally supportive, and between them William and Kate should bring sparkle and charm to the monarchy.

THE ROYAL HOMES – *Town & Country*

Like any newly married couple, Kate and William will want to enjoy a period of cosy domesticity when they return from their honeymoon. William's job, as a Search and Rescue helicopter pilot with No. 22 Squadron, is based at RAF Valley on the island of Anglesey in North Wales. There the couple already have a cottage tucked away down a remote winding lane, where they will live for the first few years, when not undertaking official engagements.

Unlike most newly-weds, the pair will have the pick of royal homes to visit and will be given a London apartment, most likely in Kensington Palace, where Prince William was brought up and where other members of the Royal Family have apartments.

They will spend time at Clarence House, the mansion built in 1825 by architect John Nash, from where Prince William and Prince Harry run their private offices. Clarence House became Prince Charles's official London residence after the death of his grandmother, who had lived there for many years. The classically proportioned stuccoed building underwent extensive renovation, using new colour schemes, fabrics and works of art chosen from The Royal Collection, before Prince Charles and his sons moved in in 2003, but the atmosphere of a much-loved family house has been skilfully maintained.

And, of course, William and Kate will be invited to Highgrove House, the country home of Prince Charles and his wife the Duchess of Cornwall. This stone house, with its neo-classical façade, once belonged to Maurice Macmillan, son of the former Prime Minister, but was bought by the Duchy of Cornwall on Prince Charles's behalf in 1980.

Left: Kensington Palace, where Prince William spent his boyhood and where the newly married couple will live when in London.

Highgrove is not a large property but it is the hub of Prince Charles's organic farms which produce ingredients for the products sold under the 'Duchy Original' label. Here is a glorious garden, designed by the late Rosemary Verey, and the famous wildflower 'meadow' planned by the late Miriam de Rothschild.

Other invitations will come from Her Majesty The Queen to visit Buckingham Palace and her country homes, Balmoral in Scotland and the beautiful Sandringham Estate in Norfolk.

The couple will also enjoy visits to Windsor Castle, said to be The Queen's favourite home and a reminder to Prince William of his schooldays at nearby Eton College.

During their long courtship William and Kate sometimes stayed at Birkhall, the secluded, whitewashed Jacobean hunting lodge on the Balmoral Estate, bequeathed to Prince Charles by his late grandmother. Kate's sister Philippa and brother James have spent time with them in this luxurious 12-bedroom country house in its wonderful Highland setting. The River Muick runs through the bottom of the two-acre (0.8 hectare) property while the flower garden, designed by the Queen Mother, has been updated by the Prince of Wales.

Above: Clarence House on the Mall is where Prince William has his private office.

Right: Windsor Castle, The Queen's favourite residence.

A FUTURE Together

O n the eve of the wedding William's grandmother, Queen Elizabeth II, may offer her grandson a dukedom, as is traditional when a prince of the royal blood marries. This will give the Prince a new title and determine how his new wife should be addressed.

Although, in theory, The Queen is able to establish a dukedom in any British dominion, it is unlikely that ties between Britain and Commonwealth countries will be strengthened by the couple becoming Duke and Duchess of Queensland or Toronto.

On the face of it, there are plenty of long-established British dukedoms to choose from. Look at the lists of characters in any of Shakespeare's history plays and you will see Dukes and Earls of Northumberland, Gloucester, Clarence, Kent, York, Albany, Surrey and Norfolk. But today many of these titles already have incumbents, while others have been suspended for a variety of reasons. Both the Prince and Kate Middleton have strong associations with St Andrews though there is already an Earl of St Andrews and the same goes for Anglesey, the island off North Wales, where they will start married life together.

Cornwall is out of the question – William's father, Prince Charles, and his wife are the Duke and Duchess of Cornwall, while the dukedom of York and the earldom of Wessex are the titles held by his uncles Andrew and Edward. The Duke of Kent is still hale and hearty while Gloucester is taken by Prince Richard, who is 19th in line of succession to the throne.

That leaves Windsor, Sussex, Albany, Clarence, Cambridge, Connaught and Cumberland. But two of these titles, Albany and Cumberland, were suspended in 1917 when their incumbents, Ernest Augustus, the Duke of Cumberland and Charles Edward, Duke of Albany backed the wrong side in wartime. Ernest Augustus, who went

Left: Royal occasions are marked by family appearances on the balcony at Buckingham Palace; Kate will soon play a part in the traditional gatherings.

Right: The newly-weds will start married life on the Isle of Anglesey in North Wales.

Below: Prince William on duty as a Search and Rescue pilot at RAF Valley.

Above: William at the controls of a Search and Rescue helicopter.

on to rule Hanover, backed Germany in the First World War, while the Duke of Albany not only sided with Germany in both world wars, but also went on to join the Nazi party. The Royal Family has a right to ask for the restoration of both these titles, but they are held by members of European royal families.

The Duke of Clarence has a marvellous ring to it. However, Shakespeare reminds us that the first duke, deemed to have committed treason during the Wars of the Roses, was drowned in a butt of Malmsey wine, while scandal dogged the footsteps of a later duke, Albert Victor, who died before his time at the age of 28 from a dose of influenza. Connaught is in Ireland now, while Windsor was the title given to King Edward VIII after he abdicated.

That leaves Sussex and Cambridge. Pundits agree that, of the two, Cambridge, with its university city rich in historical associations, is favoured and we could awake on the morning of 29 April to watch the wedding of the brand new Duke and Duchess of Cambridge.

Good wishes for William and Kate ride hand-in-hand with high hopes for the future of the British monarchy. The news that Prince William, a popular member of the Royal Family, is to marry the beautiful, clever and trustworthy Kate, has been met with immense public goodwill. Between them they could secure the long-term future of a monarchy which is in the process of modernization.

Hard lessons from the past have been learned, and the attraction and fun that the newly-wed couple will bring is being met by an institution that is coming to terms with modern expectations.

Prince William has made it known that there is no question that he might become the next King in the place of his father, the Prince of Wales. Royal aides have said that William, the heir presumptive, knows of speculation that he might succeed his grandmother to the throne. He insists, however, that Prince Charles will be the next King and has said that he has no desire to climb the ladder of kingship before his time. Both William and his brother Harry are close to Prince Charles and supportive of him and his work as Prince of Wales.

With Kate at his side, William will start married life in the relative peace and seclusion of rural Wales, working as an RAF helicopter pilot, a job he is contracted to do until at least 2013.

There will be some royal duties, but not too many, allowing the couple to ease gently into what will become an increasingly demanding life. The Prince is patron of about 20 organizations but there are no plans to increase that number in the foreseeable future, because of his commitment to his post at RAF Valley.

There is speculation about their plans to have children: both William and Kate clearly enjoy family life and both have said they want a happy family of their own.

Kate will take up her own projects as time goes on but it is clear that there is no pressure for her to be propelled into a round of public engagements before she is ready. She is wise and sensible enough to know that she will never be out of the public spotlight, but royal aides have confirmed that the plan is to introduce her carefully to the role that will be hers one day, to learn the ropes and not have to take the plunge unprepared.

William, too, will have time to prepare for kingship. He may continue with the armed services after 2013, or he might ask for secondment to government departments to learn about constitutional management.

As their future unrolls, the William and Kate story brings a new era to the Royal Family and its place in British life. When they stand at the high altar at Westminster Abbey to make their vows to each other with love and commitment, the hopes and wishes of a nation will be with them.

Above: William and Kate cheer on the England rugby team playing Italy at Twickenham in early 2007.

ACKNOWLEDGEMENTS

The coat of arms on the inside front cover is reproduced by kind permission of the College of Arms.

Photographs by kind permission of:

Alamy: FC (newsphoto), 32 34br 51tl 53tc (Trinity Mirror/Mirrorpix), 33 (Allstar Picture Library), 35tr (Jayne Fincher.Photo Int), 38 (Terry Fincher.Photo.Int), 56bl (newsphoto), 59tr (Chris Nash); **Camera Press**: 1 17t (ROTA), 3 46bl 49br 51tr 53bl & r (Mark Stewart), 12 (James Veysey), 29tr 31cl 49tl (Richard Gillard), 49tr (James Peltekian); **Getty Images**: 2 14 15 both 31t 37tr (AFP), 17cr 19 28 42 both 60 (WireImage), 22 27c 36bl 37cl 50br 53tr (Tim Graham), 26cl (Popperfoto), 36br (Time & Life Images), 40bl (for Orange) 16cr, 29tl, 30, 31cr, 34bl, 35tl, 35br, 39, 41, 46br, 47tr, 49bl, 50bl, 52, 53tl, 55, 56br, 57, 61tr, 61cr; **Pitkin Publishing**: 21 26/27b 58 (Heather Hook), 24, 25 both, 59b; **Press Association**: 13 16 BC (Kirsty Wigglesworth/AP), 63 (Alastair Grant); **Rex Features**: 27b (Eugene Adebari), 40br (Tim Rooke), 43, 45 (Stephen Lock), 47tl (Brendan Beirne) 61cl.

THIS GUIDEBOOK IS JUST ONE OF PITKIN'S COLLECTABLE SERIES ON ROYALTY AND HISTORY

Available by mail order. See our website, www.pitkin-guides.com, for our full range of titles, or contact us for a copy of our brochure.

Pitkin Publishing, Healey House, Dene Road, Andover, Hampshire SP10 2AA, UK. **Sales and enquiries:** 01264 409200 **Fax:** 01264 334110
Email: sales@thehistorypress.co.uk